Ultimate

to Machine Knitting for Beginners

Beginners

Learn to Knit Baby Blankets, Hats, Dishcloths & MORE!

Over 75 Pictures & Illustrations

By

Sophia Anderson

AUTUMN LEAF
PUBLISHING PRESS

Design & Illustration by Rebecca Johnson

First Edition

Table of Contents

Special Thanks

I would like to take a minute to thank some very special people in my life.

I dedicate this book to my daughter, Eugenia. Without her constant support, I would be lost.

I would also like to thank my mother, who instilled her love of handmade things in me as well.

Even if those "handmade" things were ultimately crafted using a machine, they were still thoughtfully designed "by hand."

Most importantly, I would like to thank you, the reader of this book.

I am so happy you are also interested in the wonderful world of knitting.

Thank you so much for purchasing and reading this book!

I am amazed at how far technology has progressed in every area of our lives to try to make things easier on a day-to-day basis.

The technology used for knitting is also no small feat. It astounds me that a machine can mimic what human hands can create.

Introduction

Knitting machines are suitable solutions for slow hand knitters who have the objective of achieving a certain finish on a deadline.

A couple of hand knitters are fast, but not all of them.

Machine knitting excludes the boredom part of knitting since the machine brings in an aspect of enthusiasm in the knitting process.

In the modern world, there are several machines made for this specific activity. Many of them are made simply so as they can be used by anybody who has a passion for knitting but is not talented in using their hands to knit.

In this guide, we are going to go through the steps that can help any interested knitter to be able to know how to choose a suitable machine. We will examine the step-by-step knitting of various patterns and finalizing the projects.

All of this will be vividly depicted with pictures. This book will be available in two formats- eBook and paperback print. The eBook will contain full-color versions of the pictures found in the paperback print version.

Types of Machines

There are many different varieties of knitting machines on the market to choose from.

Which machine you choose will depend greatly on your personal budget and which features you are comfortable using.

Plastic Bed Machines

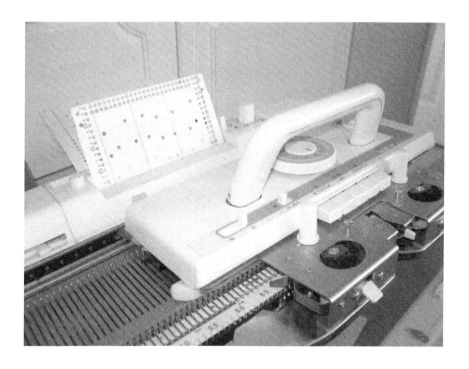

These machines are:

- Good for a beginner

- They are less complicated

- Have few accessories

- Sold at lower prices

- Usually use heavy yarns.

Metal Bed Machines

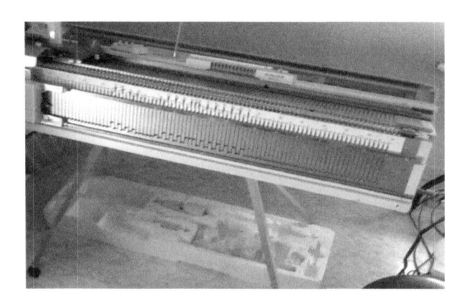

These types of machines are:

- Usually reasonably priced

- Equipped with many features

- Automated

- Electronic

- Suitable for medium gauge yarns

Electronic Machines

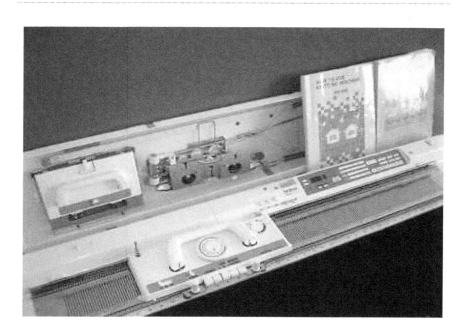

This type of machine has:

- Many automatic patterns

- Can be controlled by a computer

- Can be programmed using special software

Ribbing Attachment

These machines are:

- Flatbed machines

- Cannot produce purl stitches

- Are more tedious to operate

Knitting Basics

Some people are tight and tense. Hence their knitting tends to be tense and tight. Other people are relaxed and loose, which makes their knitting relaxed and loose.

Humans, compared to machines, have some tendencies and quirks which will eventually extend to their knitting.

Two people knitting a similar pattern using the same yarn with needles of the same size could eventually end up with pieces of very different sizes.

Knitting Gauge Explained

Typically, a knitting pattern will include instructions on the gauge that resemble this:

Gauge	10sts/15 rows	4 inches in stockinette stitch

This instruction basically dictates that if you make a knit of ten stitches for fourteen rows in stockinette stitch, the stitches should be of 4 inches in both height and width.

This is what is referred to as a gauge swatch. When a gauge swatch matches a pattern gauge, then the correct gauge for the pattern required is achieved.

Gauge in machine knitting refers to the number of needles a knitting machine has and their spacing on the needle bed.

Gauge involves three things:

- Needle size

- A person's knitting tension

- Yarn weight.

Knitting tension cannot be adjusted, as it is a unique quality in a person and is an attribute that flows from one's fingers.

It is advisable for a person to embrace their knitting tension.

Yarn weight and needle size, on the other hand, can be altered to ensure the right gauge for your pattern is achieved.

To knit a gauge swatch, one has first to select a needle size and yarn that will potentially be used for the knitting piece.

Many patterns usually have a prescribed yarn weight and needle size.

Types of Gauges on Knitting Machines

Each knitting machine is designed to deal with a range of yarns in the scope of fine to bulky.

Machine specifications stipulate the needle pitch in millimeters (mm) and give the number of needles in the machine.

There are four types of gauges among knitting machines.

Bulky Gauge

Such machines have a needle pitch of 9mm and 114 needles. Their design enables them to deal with worsted weight yarns to knit sweaters that resemble hand knits and can also be used with bulky yarns and sport weight.

Mid-Gauge

The mid-gauge machine was primarily designed to combine the bulky and standard machines.

Many of these machines, however, are of inferior quality with fewer stitch capabilities and plastic beds for the needles.

Standard Gauge

These are the most common machines in knitting. They have a needle pitch of 4.5mm and a total of 200 needles.

They can be used to sew an assortment of yarns from sport weight to lace weight. They basically sew lighter patterns compared to the bulky gauge machines.

Fine Gauge

These machines are designed to handle the finest yarns from lace weight yarns to mere threads.

They produce very fine fabrics and are mostly used in manufacturing clothing.

Understanding Basic Stitches

It's important to understand the basic knitting stitches and how they work together in order to understand what your machine is making. Let's examine the most common knitting stitches.

Seed Stitch

This type of stitch made up of purls and single knits which alternate both vertically and horizontally. It is among the most basic stitching patterns.

The bumps created by this mode of knitting resemble the shape of seeds hence the name "seed stitch."

The seed stitch has a two-row repeat knit stitch blueprint which is in essence reversible. The seed stitch has a reversible pattern, implying that both the wrong and the right sides of the stitch are identical.

There are two types of seed stitch patterns, the odd and the even patterns.

Although the seed stitch is somehow more complicated than the stockinette and garter stitches, it forms a captivating texture that has over time been included in many patterns.

A similarity between seed and garter stitch is that both lie flat, making them a great edge for cuffs and sweater borders.

When doing the seed stitch, it is important to keep in mind that the purls and knits should never create stacks on each other.

The stitch basically looks the same on both sides, and this technique can be employed in knitting scarves, blankets, hats, neckties, and sweaters.

A valley on one side is a bump on the other side, giving the final product an even feel. Since the stitch is spread flat, it is very suitable for cuffs and border sweaters.

The seed stitch is made by working one purl stitch and one knit stitch on a row.

They are eventually alternated for each and every row by purling the knit stitches and knitting the purl stitches. This creates the seed shape.

The seed stitch is similar to the British moss in some distinct ways.

To knit a seed stitch, you will need the following materials:

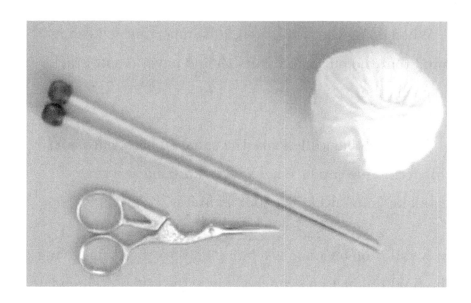

- Yarn

- Knitting needles

- A tapestry needle

- Scissors

Cast on an odd number of stitches.

Knitting Rows

Knitting on the rows shall be for both the right and the wrong side.

For the right side, *K1, P1*, K1 then repeat the pattern between the asterisks **

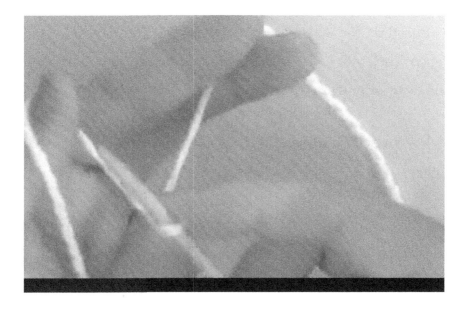

For the wrong side, *K1, P1*, K1 then repeat the pattern between the asterisks **

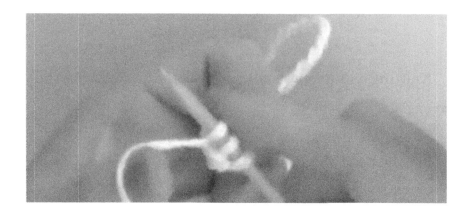

Based on the size you require (length), you have to repeat the rows (1-2) in the same manner so as to derive the desired pattern.

For an even number of stitches, the process is also as follows:

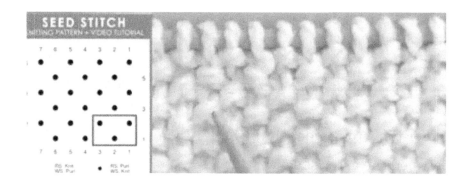

For the right side, *K1, P1*, then repeat the pattern between the asterisks **

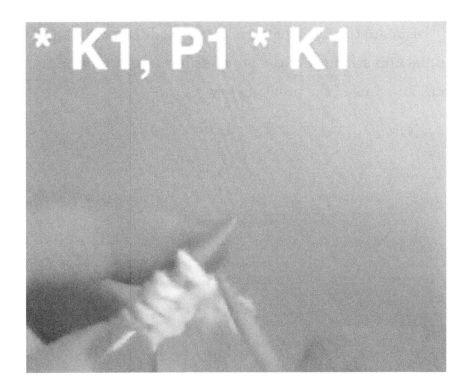

For the wrong side, *P1, K1*, then repeat the pattern between the asterisks **

Based on the length you desire, you have to repeat the rows (1-2) in the same manner so as to achieve the desired pattern.

Note

When operating with the seed stitch model, you have to interchange between purl and knit in each of the rows of your stitching.

To create the 'seed' pattern in this mode of sewing, purl in the knit stitching of the previous row and to knit in the purl stitching of the previous row.

Bee Stitch

This stitch is classified as a "Brioche" knit. It is very similar to the honeycomb brioche.

This means that it is fluffy and light and has a great dimension.

The bee stitch can be very effective in knitting hats, scarves, sweaters, knit neckties, dishcloths, pillows, and even blankets.

Note

The edges in a bee stitch do not roll over, making it different from a garter stitch.

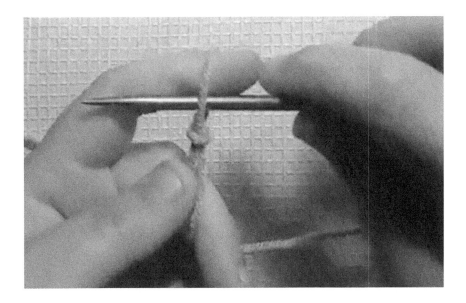

The bee stitch is comprised of 2 stitches combined with 1 over 4 rows.

For this particular stitch, you are required to have an odd number of stitches.

The technique described below will give this pattern a very unique texture.

Materials

To knit a bee stitch, you will require the following materials:

- Worsted weight yarn and knitting needle of your preferred size.

- Yarn in any fiber, weight and in the color of your liking

- Tapestry needle

- Scissors

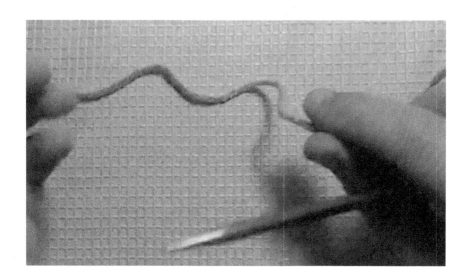

Instructions

Slot in a needle into the stitch exactly beneath the next stitch on the needle.

Next, wrap and knit the piece as it is normally done. This will allow the stitch to fall off on the left needle side.

Cast on an odd number of stitches.

In this particular bee stitch, there are four rows.

You will continue on these four rows until you have achieved the length you need for the final product is achieved.

The entire row one is to be stitched.

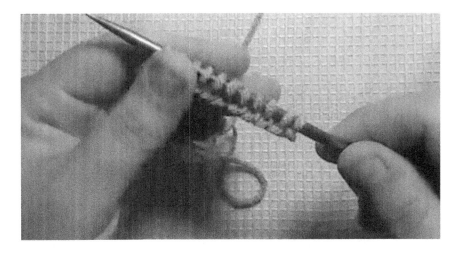

As for row 2, *K1B, K1* and then repeat between the asterisks.

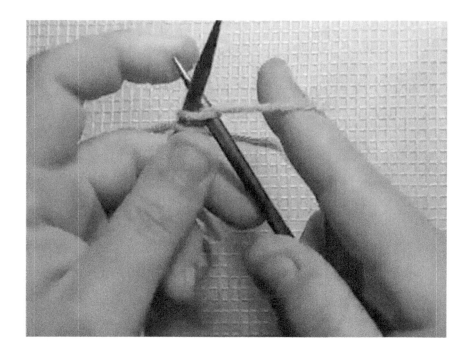

The entire of row three is also to be stitched as row one.

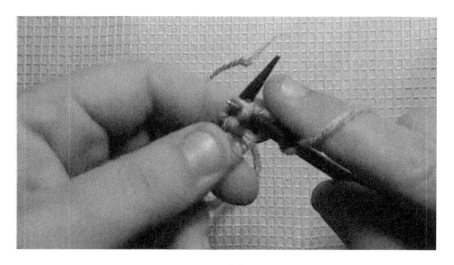

In row 4, K2, K1B, *K1, K1B*

The four rows should be repeated in the same manner until you achieve the length you desire. After completing these steps, you have made a bee stitch.

Brioche Stitch

The term 'brioche' is a general term that is used to refer to a myriad of stitching that is done in the same way.

The elements of a brioche stitch comprise of a slip stitch and a yarn over which are knitted together on the other row.

Although garments made using the brioche technique are beautiful and warm in texture, they have the possible disadvantage that the stitches tucked could get caught and pulled out.

Brioche knitting originated from the Middle East. The term "brioche" itself is believed to have originated from the French where it is slang for "mistake."

This is in reference to a dinner roll made using the brioche technique and is comprised of two parts - one resting on the other.

It takes two passes to complete one row of knitting in a brioche stitch because only half of the stitches get knitted each time.

The other remaining half of stitches are slipped off.

Due to this, it is difficult to count the stitches and rows and gauge measurement.

Variations of the Brioche Stitch

The brioche stitch has very many different variations. There are some variations that work with an even number of stitches but do not involve the use of a yarn over at the start of the row so as to produce a smoother edge for the finished product.

Other variations of the brioche stitch adopt a two-row repeat, although technically, they are usually considered to be of the same row.

To understand the brioche knitting technique completely, one can start with a swatch attempting to create a basic pattern such as a Stripped Brioche Stitch Hot Pad.

This particular pattern is designed in a way that two rows are a repeat of one row.

The first row of this pattern, however, is unique and thus not repeated in the stitching.

Brioche stitches exist in many separate forms such as:

- Waffle brioche

- Double brioche

- Fisherman's rib

- Various other techniques.

The syncopated Bri Fisherman's Rib has some similarities with the Brioche and is even occasionally referred to as a brioche technique.

Technically, it is not a brioche technique since it does not have yarn overs and slipped stitches, which are the very bedrock of a brioche stitching.

Instead, the syncopated Bri Fisherman's Rib has stitches that have been worked inside the row below to produce the puffy and distinctive look of brioche.

The brioche stitch pattern can be quite intimidating when learning it, but once you get the hang of it, it becomes a piece of cake.

How the Brioche Stitch is Knitted

The brioche works with an even number of stitches.

The stitches get slipped as if purling them with the yarn at the completion of the stitching.

For row 1, *yarn over and slip 1, knit 1 then repeat from * across

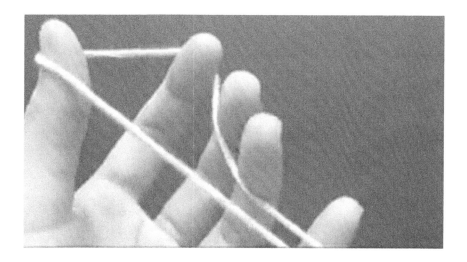

For row 2, * yarn over and slip 1, knit 2 together then repeat from * across.

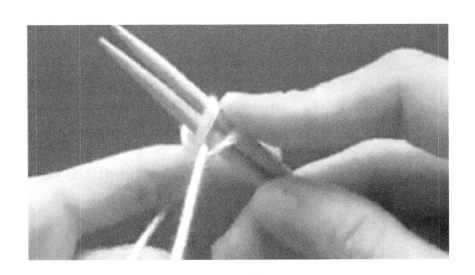

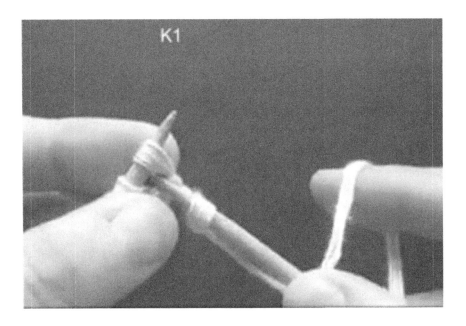

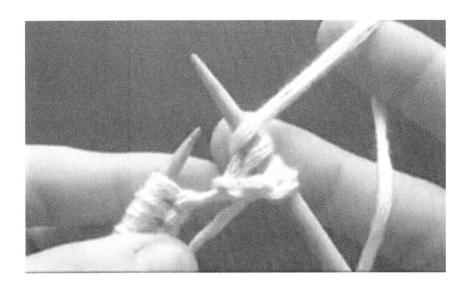

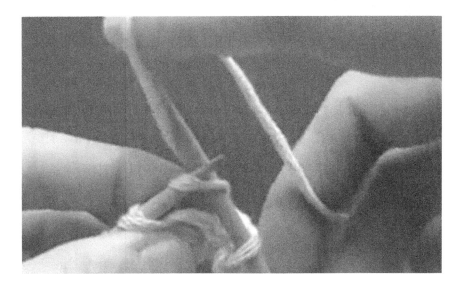

For the pattern to be created, you will have to repeat only row two.

You should note that the preparation row will require you to work with more stitches than the ones to be cast on.

This should be adequately planned for when one is determining the gauge.

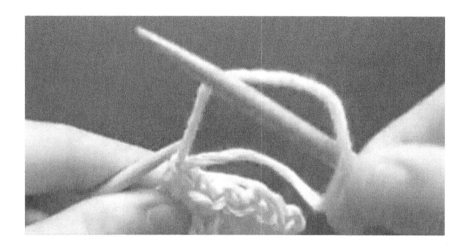

When completing knitting, especially the ribbing area in brioche at the cuff or hem of a cloth, seek to eliminate the yarn overs in that row and purl the knitting across together.

After accomplishing this, you can finish off with the regular purl 1, knit 1 ribbing pattern.

The binding should also be left loose due to the stretchy nature of the fabric.

Teardrop Stitch

The teardrop stitch is a lovely design, especially when used for baby sweaters or blankets.

For an intermediate knitter looking to take up some time knitting, the teardrop stitch is the perfect go-to as it integrates the techniques and combinations of knitted stitches to generate the desired outcome.

At first instance, an end product of the teardrop stitch may seem to have been created using a yarn over. In reality, the entire pattern is created from strategically timed increases and decreases.

A faux yarn over is first created by generating 5 stitches from one original stitch, which create space in the original stitch. This is referred to as the hole, which is the base of the 'teardrop' shape.

Left and right leaning will then decrease the stand out against a reverse stockinet or background in the long run, framing the rest of the teardrop shape.

The teardrop pattern is worked by a multiple of 4 stitches, with another extra one across 13 rows. Due to the fact that the pattern is offset in each row, thirteen rows will create a complete one and a half teardrop shape.

Abbreviations

The abbreviations used in the pattern are:

- CO means to cast on

- K means to knit

- P means to purl

- Ssk means slip slip knit

- Sl 1 is to slip 1 stitch knitwise on the right needle

- K2tog means to knit two stitches

Instructions

The written pattern for a teardrop stitch is:

CO twenty-one stitches (or any other number of stitches that is a multiple of 4 plus one)

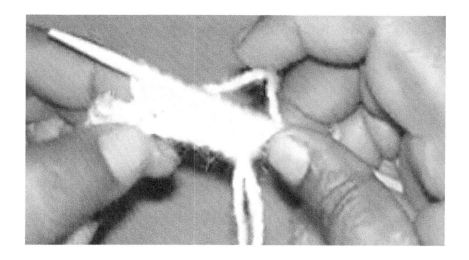

For row 1 on the right side, P1, *(K1, P1, K1, P1, K1) for the next stitch, p3, repeat from * asterisks to the end.

For row 2, *K3,p5, then redo from * asterisks to the end.

For row three, P1, *k5, p3 then repeat from *asterisks to the finish.

For row 4, *K3, p5 then repeat from *asterisks to k1, which is the last stitch.

For row 5, P1, *slip, slip then knit, k1, knit two stitches, P3 then redo from * asterisks to the end.

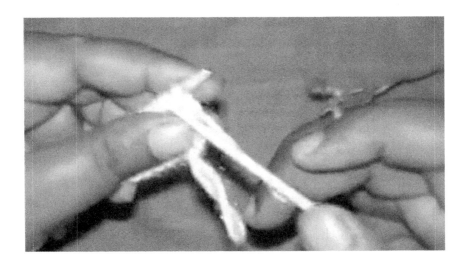

For row 6, *K3, p3, then repeat from the * to the finish.

For row 7, P1, *sl1, K2tog, psso, P1, (k1, p1, k1, p1, k1) for the next stitch, P1 then redo from * to the finish.

For row 8, K1, *p5, k3 then repeat from the asterisks to the end.

As for row nine, *P3, k5, then repeat from * the asterisks to the end, st p1.

For row 10, K1, *p5, k3 then repeat from the asterisks to the end.

For row 11, *P3, ssk, k1, k2tog then repeat from * to the last stitch, p1.

For row 12, K1, *p3, k3 then repeat from * asterisks to the end.

For row 13, P1, *(k1, p1, k1, p1, k1) for the next stitch, p1, sl 1, k2tog, psso, p1 then repeat from * to the end.

You then repeat rows 2-13.

Bind off the pattern at row 7 or 13. This omits the increases from these rows as the stitches are bound.

Fisherman Scalloped Baby Blanket

With the small size of infants, the fisherman scalloped baby blanket pattern ranges from 18 to 22 square inches. The pattern described below was made using a Passap Duo 80.

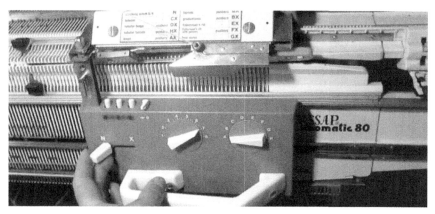

The tucked rib gives the blanket thickness, and there is also the factor that it is identical on both sides. This blanket can also be made using a Japanese flatbed machine.

For this pattern, high-quality acrylic was used. This specific yarn knits the fisherman scalloped baby blanket pattern with a 4.5/4.5 tension, and the finished baby blanket is 20 by 22 inches.

Instructions

Cast 100 needles on both beds.

Handle down the orange strippers.

Keep in mind the needle rule- that the needle on the rightmost should be on the back bed while the needle on the leftmost is on the front bed.

Ensure that the pushers are in rest.

Lock the machine on the right.

Knit one row to the left with N/N tension 4.5/4.5

Knit two rows with CX/CX tension 3.5/3.5

Knit one row to the right with N/N tension 4.5/4.5

The cast on is now complete.

Next, lock the machine onto the right.

Rack the first bed with a full turn to the left (Row count 000).

With EX/EX tension 4.5/4.5, knit a single row to the left.

Rack the first bed with a full turn to the right.

Knit a single row to the right.

Repeat the two rows 7 times (Row Count 014).

Knit an additional row without racking (Row count 015).

Repeat the 15 rows.

Rack a complete turn to the left, knit a single row.

Rack a complete turn to the right, knitting one row a total of 7 times.

Finish the pattern by knitting one row minus the racking. At this point, you should have a Row Count of 030.

Depending on the size you desire for your blanket, repeat these 30 rows.

For this blanket, the row count reached 479, with the 480th row completed using a laxer tension of 6/6 which made it easy to complete a bind off.

For the last row, switch to N/N from EX/EX for easier stitching of the remainder of the tucked stitches.

For those who might find a latching bind of using the machine, you can switch to CX/CX on a waste yarn and perform several knits before removing the blanket from the machine. After this, remove the waste yarn and latch the live stitches.

Tips for Achieving the Perfect Rack

The tick marks on the racking scale are imperative in determining the end product of your knitting. Make sure to write them down and do not rely upon your memory.

Your knitting will basically tell you if you racked correctly. Remember that at the end of a row, the yarn flows naturally from the last needle adjacent to the lock.

When this is not the case, then you have not succeeded in getting your desired rack.

Before you start to knit, make sure to create a table indicating the rows. This will show the contents of the row counter before you knit transition rows which normally are knitted minus the racking.

For instance:

The row counter shows the row numbers before the transition rows knit without the racking.

0-30 14 29	241-270 254 269
31-60 44 59	271-300 284 299
61-90 74 89	301-330 314 329
91-120 104 119	331-360 344 359

121-150 134 149	361-390 374 389
151-180 164 179	391-420 404 419
181-210 194 209	421-450 434 449
211-240 224 232	451-480 464 479

Fisherman's Rib Reversible Cable Stitch

For double-sided crosses, the full fisherman's rib can provide excellent results.

Side 1

This is an example of what the fisherman's rib looks like. You can see three rows of crosses on this one side of the pattern.

Fisherman's rib and the reversible cable stitch can be knit with either a Passap machine or the Brother Studio silver reed machine with ribber.

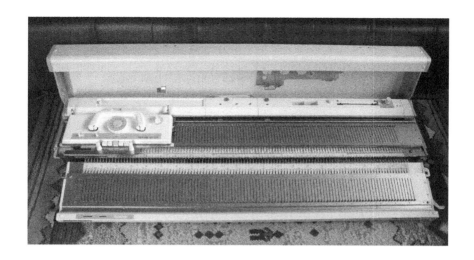

The full fisherman's rib is basically created by inserting one bed while you knit the other and then doing the reverse process when passing through again.

You will need to select an odd number of the repeats to be knitted between the crosses.

Side 2

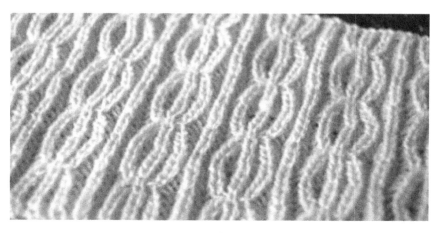

One can easily spot the four rows created by the crosses.

In this demonstration, I used 9 rows that pass in between the crosses.

The shown sample was knitted using a Passap Duo 80.

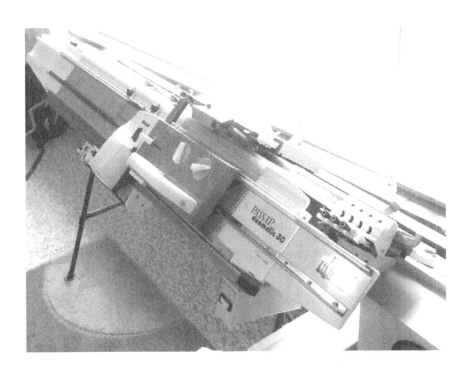

Instructions

The process is as follows:

First, cast on.

After you have cast on, ensure that both of the locks are set to EX/EX.

With this preset, knit 9 rows.

On the bed that has knit stitches, make a crossing of the stitches.

Again, knit 9 rows.

Now cross the stitches that you have just knitted on the opposite bed.

Repeat this process until you achieve your desired length.

How to Cross the Cables.

For this fisherman's rib sample, the knit was made with a full needle rib set up where each and every needle on the bed was used in the knitting.

Beginning from the right side, on the bed of the stitch that needs to be crossed, number the needles mentally so that you do not get confused during the crossing.

Numbering can be as such, "1, 2, 3, 4 - 1, 2, 3, 4," as you proceed to the left.

Then, skipping needle 1, remove the stitch on needle 2 and stitch it onto the transfer tool.

Then skip needle 3, placing the stitch that you have removed from needle 4 on a separate transfer tool.

The next step is to place the stitch on needle 2 onto the stitch on needle 4 and then place the needle 4 stitch onto the needle 2.

This process should be repeated across the bed.

Knit using the above-stated procedure for 9 rows.

Repeat the patterns you have knitted on the bed opposite beginning from the right side of the machine bed.

Then finally, knit another 9 rows.

A Simple Machine Knit Hat Pattern

Knitting a hat is said to be among the easiest patterns one can knit.

For starters, the entire process does not make it necessary that you have a ribber.

For this pattern, you simply knit a square, fold the resultant square in half, and sew the open side.

Then gather the ends of the fabric and put one end inside the other.

Finally, fasten the tops of the fabric together and make sure to fold the bottom. Folding the bottom creates an extra cuff layer over the ears.

Below are instructions on how to knit a simple hat using both a bulky gauge machine and a standard gauge machine.

The Bulky Gauge Machine

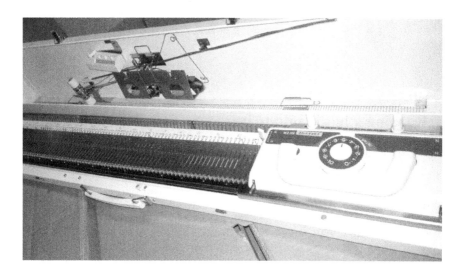

First of all, set a tension from 7 to 9 with worsted weight yarn.

The second step is to cast on each and every needle on the machine in over 75 to 85 stitches.

Knit 4 rows

At this stage, you will need to add the needles you had not cast on to start knitting.

Depending on gauge, knit between 120 to 140 rows.

At this point, you now have to transfer all the stitches to all the needles the knit for 4 rows.

Gather off the stitches with the double-eyed needle.

Make sure that you have left some sufficient yarn as this will be very important when sewing up the up side seam.

Then sew up both sides of the fabric to form a tube-like structure.

Gather the ends to the tube and join them together.

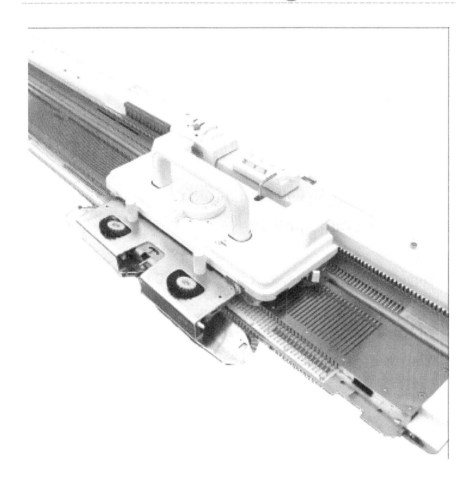

The first step is to set the tension. For this machine, the tension is set from between 7 to 9 just like in the bulky gauge machine.

Secondly, every needle is cast on between 150 to 170 stitches.

Depending on gauge, knit 200 to 220 rows.

The stitches are then transferred to every other needle.

Knit another 4 rows.

Gather of the fabric with the double eye needle.

Make sure that you have left some sufficient yarn as this will be very important when sewing up the up side seam.

Then sew up both sides of the fabric to form a tube-like structure.

Gather the ends to the tube and join them together.

Notes

For my example, I knitted 40 rows in white, another 40 rows with varied colors, and another 40 in white, in a period of less than an hour.

"Gather both ends and join together" is a step that will happen when the fabric you made has already been removed from the machine and sewn the side seam which forms the "tube" using your hands.

The loose thread that you made through the remaining stitches when the fabric was removed from the machine is then pulled.

Both the threads on the top and the corresponding bottom should be pulled so that each of them cinches their respective sides.

After this, manually shove an end of the tube of the hat into the other so that your form the required double thickness.

Lace Circular Doily Dish Rag Pattern

Considering the size, you want your doily to eventually be, cast on 12 to 18 stitches with waste yarn (yarn you plan on throwing away later).

When knitting the lace circular doily dishrag pattern, the gauge or the type of machine you choose to use is not of much importance.

Once you have finished making your pattern, you can decrease or increase any combination of stitches that you have cast on, the tension setting, yarn thickness, or the gauge of the machine to either enlarge or decrease the dish rag.

Make sure to choose a tension that is most suited for the yarn you have chosen. For those who intend to use the outcome for the purpose of a dishrag, cotton yarn will be the best-recommended yarn to use.

Instructions

For this sample, 15 stitches were cast on the yarn.

For easy monitoring of the lace increases, you need to cast needles 1 to 15 left of center.

After knitting a few rows with the waste yarn, you hang a weight at each end of the knitting.

You then remove the waste yarn and install the main yarn.

At this point, your row count is still 000

Carriage is on the right to the start.

Row 1 and 2

Place the carriage to hold.

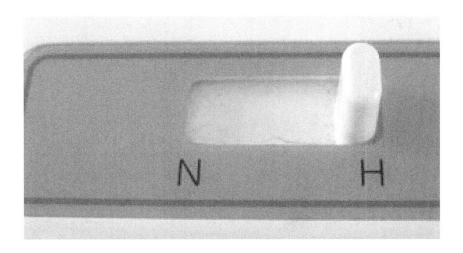

On the left-hand side, adjust the left needle to fit into position.On the right-hand side, move 3 stitches one step to the right using the three-prong transfer tool.

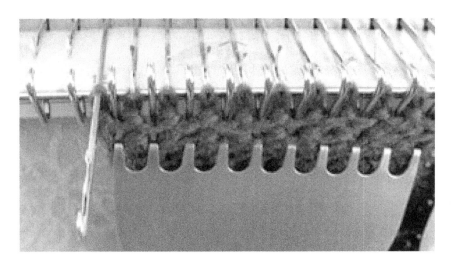

The empty needle should be left in work position. Knit two rows (Row Count 2). Carriage is on the right.

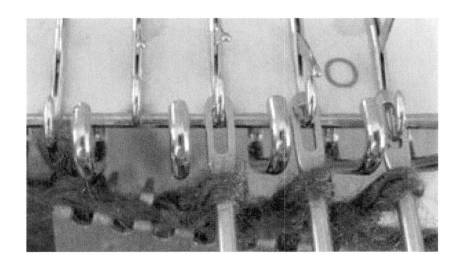

Row 3 and 4

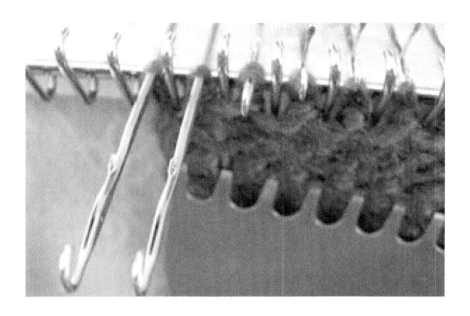

On the left-hand side, adjust the left needle to fit into position.

At this point, you have 2 needles in hold.

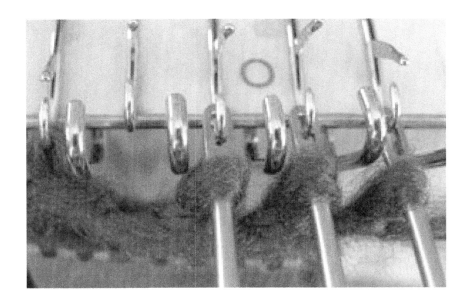

On the right-hand side, move the 3 stitches one step to the right.

Knit two rows (Row Count 4). Carriage is on the right.

Row 5 and 6

On the left-hand side, adjust the left needle to fit into position.

At this point, you have 3 needles in hold. On the right-hand side, move the 3 stitches one step to the right.

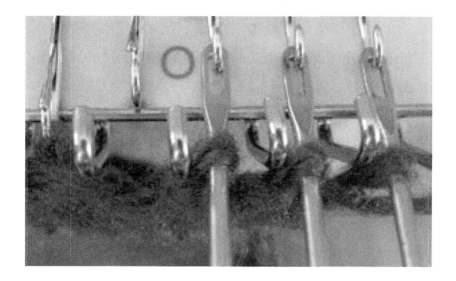

The empty needle should be left in its work position. Knit 2 rows (Row Count 006). Carriage is on the right.

Row 7 and 8

On the left-hand side, adjust the left needle to fit into position.

You now have four needles in hold.

At this point, you will not move the stitches to from race holes.

Rather, bind off the three stitches that have been added to the right side.

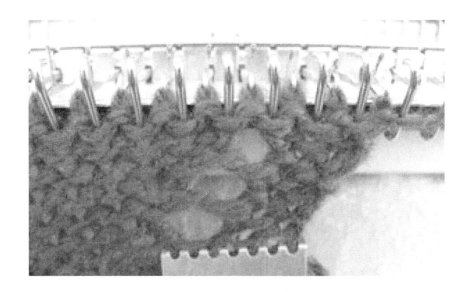

Make sure to affirm your progress by taking a step back to look at your knitting. You should be able to see the three lace holes in the current section. Add on extra yarn. Hold the extra yarn with a clip if need be.

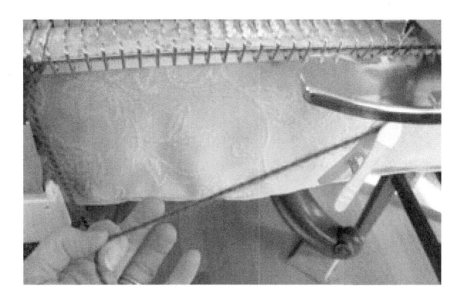

Now bind off the 3 stitches far to the right around the gate pegs using the latch tool, performing a left to right movement. The loop from the third stitch that has just been bound off is then attached to the nearby needle.

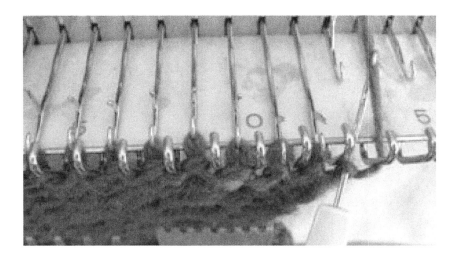

This means that you should have two stitches on one needle.

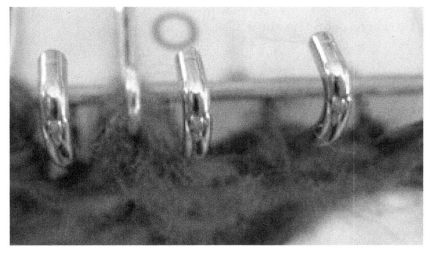

To maintain an even tension, keep the stitches that have been bound off wrapped on the gate pegs.

Now knit 2 rows (Row Count 008).

Carriage is on the right.

You can now remove the bound off stitches from the gate pegs and let them hang loose.

Continue this pattern for the lacy points. Count the needles on hold from the left side until you have a total of 11 needles on hold.

Row 9 and 10

On the left-hand side, adjust the left needle to fit into position. You now have five needles in hold.

On the right-hand side, move the 3 stitches one step to the right. The empty needle should be left in work position.

Knit for 2 rows (Row Count 010).

Carriage is on the right.

Row 11 and 12

On the left-hand side, adjust the left needle to fit into position. You now have six needles in hold.

On the right-hand side, move the 3 stitches one step to the right. The empty needle should be left in work position.

Knit for 2 rows (Row Count 012).

Carriage is on the right.

Row 13 and 14

On the left-hand side, adjust the left needle to fit into position. You now have seven needles in hold.

On the right-hand side, move the 3 stitches one step to the right. The empty needle should be left in work position.

Knit for 2 rows (Row Count 014)

Carriage is on the right.

Row 15 and 16

On the left-hand side, adjust the left needle to fit into position. You now have eight needles in hold.

The three stitches you have added to the right side are then bound off. Hang the loop from the stitch that was bound off the third to a nearby needle. This needle will now have three stitches.

Knit 2 rows (Row Count 016).

Carriage is on the right.

Remove the three stitches that were bound off and let them hang loose.

Row 17 and 18

On the left-hand side, adjust the left needle to fit into position. You now have nine needles in hold.

On the right-hand side, move the 3 stitches one step to the right. The empty needle should be left in work position.

Knit for 2 rows. (Row Count 018)

Carriage is on the right.

Row 19 and 20

On the left-hand side, adjust the left needle to fit into position. You now have ten needles in hold.

On the right-hand side, move the 3 stitches one step to the right. The empty needle should be left in work position.

Knit for 2 rows. (Row Count 020).

Carriage is on the right.

Row 21 and 22

On the left-hand side, adjust the left needle to fit into position. You now have eleven needles in hold.

On the right-hand side, move the 3 stitches one step to the right. The empty needle should be left in work position.

Knit for 2 rows (Row Count 022).

Carriage is on the right.

Row 23 and 24

For this row, you don't do anything on the left side as you have eleven needles on hold.

The three stitches you have added to the right side are then bound off. Hang the loop from the stitch that was bound off the third to a nearby needle. This needle will now have three stitches.

To maintain an even tension, keep the stitches that have been bound off wrapped on the gate pegs.

You can now turn carriage hold off.

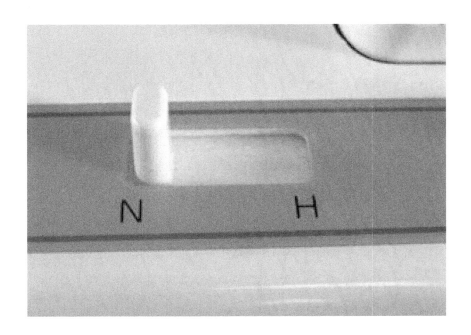

Knit 2 rows (Row Count 24).

Carriage is on the right.

Remove the three stitches that were bound off and let them hang loose.

Replicate rows 1 to 24 until you create enough wedges for the formation of a circle. This sample took 6 repeats of the 24 rows.

When you achieve your desired size, use the Kitchener stitch to weave the two sides together.

Tuck Stitch Reversible Baby Blanket

Step 1

Bring out the needles for casting on.

To achieve a symmetrical look, 47 needles were used for the front and 46 needles for the back.

This will allow for 5 and a half pattern repeats and an additional stitch on each front edge. This method ensures the stitches that have been tucked in do not fall off.

This also implies that the vertically scalloped edges are not staggering since each side of the mini blanket will end in either a square or a fisherman's tuck square.

Step 2

Tubular Cast-on.

For those who wish to abide by the Passap needle rule (that the rightmost needle should be on the back bed), cast on 46 stitches on both the beds.

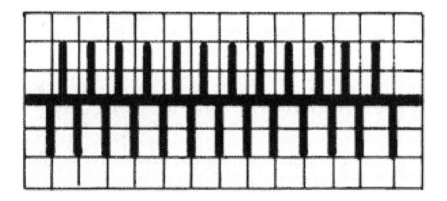

When you are done, bring out an extra front needle on the right and put a purl bump onto it before you perform step 3.

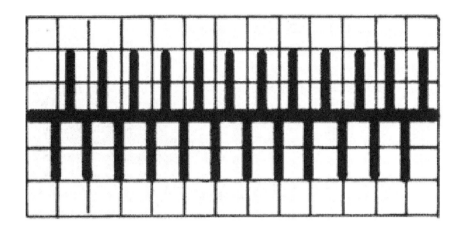

Different steps were used for the two separate knits - lavender cotton blend sample and the green fingerling wool sample.

Lavender Cotton Blend Variation

Follow these steps:

1. Lock onto the right.

2. Put the racking handle down.

3. Orange strippers.

4. Tension 1.5 N/N Knit one row.

5. Tension 3.75 CX/CX Knit two rows.

6. Tension 5.0 N/N Knit one row.

Green Fingerling Wool Variation

Use these steps:

1. Lock onto the right.

2. Put the racking handle down.

3. Orange strippers.

4. Tension 1.5 N/N Knit one row.

5. Tension 3.25 CX/CX Knit two rows.

6. Tension 4.5 N/N Knit one row.

Step 3

Creating the bottom border rows.

When you complete the cast on, knit 4 additional rows in a full needle rib. Complete it with a lock at the right.

This completes the bottom border of the swatch.

For the lavender swatch, slowly increase the tension from 5 to 5.25, and 5.5 to 6.0, with each of these passes so that by the end of the 4th N/N row, your tension is at 6.0.

For the other sample, maintain a tension of 4.5 throughout.

Step 4

Arrange pattern needles and pushers.

After completing the bottom border, arrange the needles and pushers as demonstrated in the diagram.

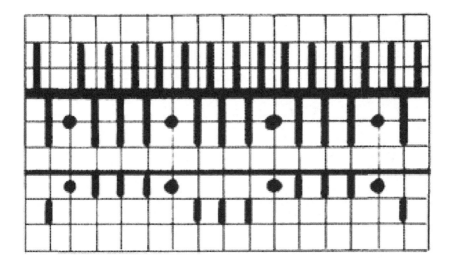

With the racking handle down, manually put down the right and left most pushers.

Knit 2 rows N/<-FX release the left arrow key, knit 8 rows N/FX repeat those 10 rows.

Continue with the same pattern until you reach a row count of 10.

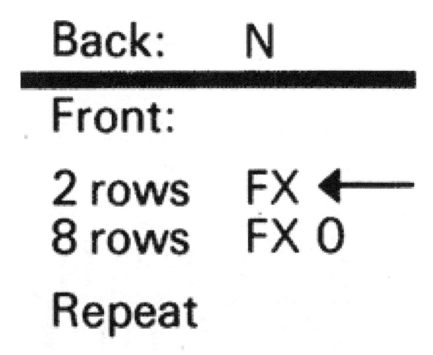

At the beginning of the first <-FX row, remember to lower the right manually, and the leftmost pushers.

Before you knit row 11, repeat this process, lowering the leftmost and the rightmost pushers on the front bed.

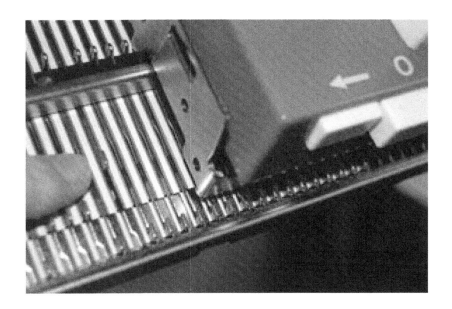

The reasoning for this is to ensure that the edge stitches knit and don't tuck. It basically gives a very neat edge that rolls gently to the back.

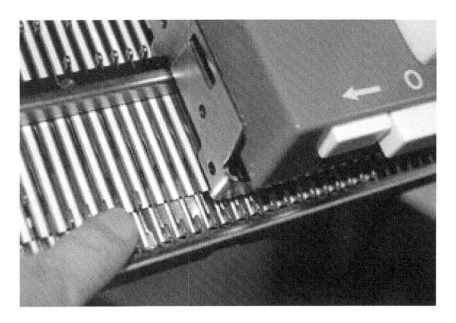

Step 5

Handling the top border rows.

Pull up the purl bumps to fill in for the full needle rib at the front bed.

Lock onto the right

N/N Knit 3 rows ending the lock on the left.

Step 6

Tubular cast-off.

Come to a full stop!

Transfer the stitch on the front right to the back needle so that there is an even number of stitches on the back and front beds. The final stitch ends on the right of the back bed.

There are different steps for both the lavender cotton blend sample and the green fingerling wool sample.

Lavender Cotton Blend Alternate Instructions

1. Lock on the left

2. With a tension of 5.0 N/N Knit 2 rows.

3. Transfer the stitch on the rightmost side of the front bed to the back bed.

4. With a tension of 3.75 CX/CX Knit two rows.

5. Make sure not to cut the main yarn.

Green Fingerling Wool Alternate Instructions

1. Lock onto the left.

2. With a tension of 4.5 N/N Knit two rows.

3. Transfer the stitch on the rightmost side of the front bed to the back bed.

4. With a tension of 3.25 CX/CX Knit two rows

5. Make sure not to cut the main yarn

Step 7

Half tubular waste knitting.

Lock BX->/BX->

Black strippers.

Put the racking handle up.

Arrange the pushers and needles in the manner demonstrated in this diagram.

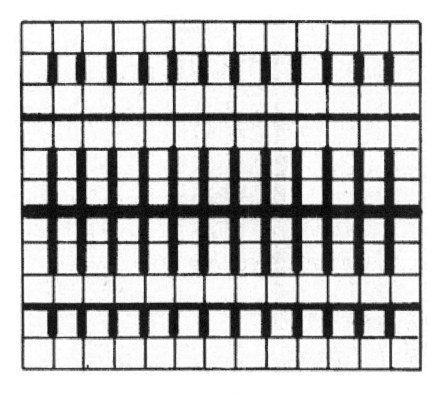

For the front bed, the pushers should be in working position. On the back bed, they are put in the rest position.

Knit for 6 rounds then remove.

Step 8

Weave end stitches.

For a tubular cast-off, use the Kitchener stitch to sew the back and front stitches together.

Pull out a length of the main yarn that is at least three times the width of the finished blanket, starting at the end when the main yarn tail is.

When you are done with this, take a measurement of your swatch to establish how many rows long and how many stitches wide you will require for your baby blanket.

Cable Baby Blanket Pattern

Cable baby blanket patterns are super cute and fun to make.

Below are the instructions of making a cable baby blanket pattern using a machine.

Note

First of all, the machine used to sew this pattern is the ribbed Brother 260 Bulky, T 7-9, depending on your chosen yarn.

To accommodate the cabling, you will need to set the machine looser than you would for a yarn knit stockinette.

Instructions

First of all, set the ribber to half pitch. With a raised waste yarn and ribber, cast on a multiple of 9 + 1 and end the stitch in a full needle rib.

Rearrange your needles as provided in the diagram.

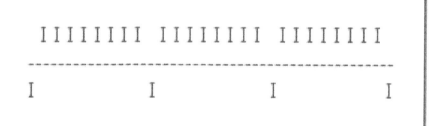

This will double up the stitches wherever they may be needed.

Knit a few rows with some waste yarn, then end the carriage on the left (Row Count 000).

Now turn to the main yarn.

Following the first pattern once:

K 2 rows.

Transfer the stitches by hand for Row 3 and K.

K4 more rows.

If the crosses turn out too tight, you will be required to bring one or two ribber needles up into working positions per group of cabled stitches, one row before the crossed row.

With these added, you now cross the stitches as shown (Row Count 008).

Now cross the stitches manually as per pattern 2, knitting 6 rows after each shift, including the crossed rows.

Replicate pattern 2 for the desired blanket length.

When the baby blanket reaches your desired length, cross the stitches manually as per pattern 3.

Knit the cross row and an additional 2 rows to complete pattern 3.

Now turn to the waste yarn. Knit some rows and remove the baby blanket for the machine.

Use a crotchet latch or hook to latch the last two loops in the chain. Begin this process at the opposite end where the main yarn is still joined.

Repeat the process of casting off on the cast on end so that the two ends turn out identical. This will give the blanket a ruffled look.

For those who prefer crossing cables on the front of the bed, they can follow the directions of the opposite cable.

Knit on right side – stitch located on main or back bed

Purl on right side – stitch located on ribber or front bed

Cable 2 left – using two 2 needle transfer tools, remove stitches from main bed hooks. Place left hand stitches in right hooks first. Place right hand stitches in left hooks second.

Cable 2 right – using two 2 needle transfer tools, remove stitches from main bed hooks. Place right hand stitches in left hooks first. Place left hand stitches in right hooks second.

Completing the Piece

It would indeed be great if our knitting projects could be finished once we bind off.

Even the simplest knitting pattern, however, has at least two ends that will need to be woven together.

The only exception for finishing off a piece is with knitting a horizontal scarf, where its ends are used as a fringe.

Weaving in ends, adding and blocking embellishments, are among the few things you might want to think about doing before your knitting project can be considered finished.

The following are some of the ways to finish up your knitting project.

Weaving in Ends

There are many techniques that have been employed when weaving in ends.

Some individuals prefer to weave into edges.

Some people prefer to follow the knit stitch as if creating a similar stitch.

Others choose to work in the same direction.

As time progresses, it is easier to discover the method you prefer to use to weave and finish your knitting project.

Blocking

Blocking in knitting is a step that is often skipped as it is not always necessary.

For projects such as garments, it is imperative to block them as it makes the other finishing tasks easier.

This step is essential when lace knitting.

Blocking helps smooth the rough outer edges, except for the stockinette curl.

This step makes your knitting look somewhat even and reduces the minor sizing issues you might have encountered during knitting.

Blocking does not, however, cure all your problems. In fact, when overdone, the garment may ultimately look stressed and overworked.

Using a soft hand during blocking could prove beneficial.

Seaming

When working on a garment, or any other knitting project with seams, sewing those seams will be the step that stands between you and finishing the project.

There are various ways you can go about to complete your seaming.

Ideally, different skills are applied when dealing with different types of seams.

The most common means, however, is using a mattress stitch.

This mostly applies to when you are seaming a basic stockinette stitch.

Adding Closures and Other Details

At this point in your project, you may consider sewing on buttons, lining the project, adding zippers, or creating some other addition that makes your project look complete.

You may decide to crochet the edges of your project to give it that finished look.

You may also add some embellishments or embroidery altogether.

At this point, you can also add pom-poms, fringe, and tassels.

Conclusion

I hope this book has helped you to understand further how best to use your wonderous knitting machine.

With the right patterns in hand, you can make some truly lovely designs with your chosen machine. These gifts will be cherished for years to come.

I love creating handmade products- from hats and blankets to more intricate patterns. In this book, we looked at the types of machines, what the basic knitting terms and stitches are, and I shared with you six nifty machine patterns.

If this book has helped you, please consider leaving me a review wherever you purchased this book. I would love to make more books on this subject, and I value your comments.

I hope your knitting machine is less complicated to work than it seemed initially. With this book's help, you should be making cool new crafts in no time!

Happy Creating!

Made in the USA
Las Vegas, NV
14 November 2024